Advance Praise for

Smoke Memories offers a profound meditation on how we carry our pasts within us—memories lingering like smoke, echoing in the mind, growing in the roadside weeds, embodied by the very landscapes in which we have lived our lives. Lucid and grave, lush and magical, *Smoke Memories* is a great book of poems.

—Christopher Salerno, author of *The Man Grave*

In *Smoke Memories*, Doug Ramspeck injects his adult self into past experiences to reevaluate them with a keen knowledge of mortality in mind. *My dead are sitting with me again this morning on my back porch and saying nothing*, Ramspeck explains. We must say to ourselves what the dead might wish to say. A most tender and profoundly moving new collection.

—A. Molotkov, author of *Future Symptoms*

A masterful meditation on family tragedies and grief, Doug Ramspeck's *Smoke Memories* is at turns incantatory and stark, allegorical and personal. With the titular smoke appearing as a cigarette, housefire, beekeeping tool, chimney exhaust, crematorium signal, and more, Ramspeck weaves together repeated elements that make the book feel novelistic . . . though with a language that sings, like the dream-father in "Mud Gospel": "And sometimes his voice was a cadence and a drum and a gospel, / and sometimes the words perched with the crows or muscled / out on their bellies with the snakes."

—Lisa Ampleman, author of *Mom in Space*

Other Books by Doug Ramspeck

Dancing in their Dead Mother's Dresses, stories, forthcoming
Blur, poems
Book of Years, poems
Under Black Leaves, novella
Distant Fires, poems/prose/drama
Black Flowers, poems
The Owl That Carries Us Away, stories
Original Bodies, poems
Mechanical Fireflies, poems
Possum Nocturne, poems
Where We Come From, poems
Black Tupelo Country, poems

Smoke Memories

Doug Ramspeck

Hickory, NC
2025

Smoke Memories

Copyright © 2025 Doug Ramspeck

All rights reserved. No part of this publication may be reproduced, distributed, or transmitted in any form or by any means, including photocopying, recording, or other electronic or mechanical methods, without the prior written permission of the publisher, except in the case of brief quotations embodied in critical reviews and certain other noncommercial uses permitted by copyright law. For permission requests, write to the publisher, addressed "Attention: Permissions Coordinator," at the address below.

ISBN: 978-1-959346-85-2 (Paperback)

Library of Congress Control Number: 2025931639

Cover Design by Doug Rampspeck
Cover Layout by Erin Mann
Interior Design by Robert Canipe
Author Photo by Lee Sutton-Rampseck
Cover photo from Shutterstock by Maxim van Asseldonk

Printed in the United States of America.

First printing 2025.

Redhawk Publications
The Catawba Valley Community College Press
2550 Hwy 70 SE
Hickory NC 28602
https://redhawkpublications.com

for Beth and Lee

CONTENTS

Introduction by Christopher Salerno   9

Tomato Divination   11

Part One

Orchard of Years   15
song to a raccoon on its back at the roadside   17
the midwest has a few beers before church   18
Miscarried Moon   19
Shortsightedness   20
Horses in the Fog   21
untitled oracle   22
My Father, Drunk, Shakes the Apple Boughs   23
prayer for all the drunks to be our fathers   24
the midwest sheds its skin   25
green snake reliquary   26
field oracle   27
Fourteen Omens in Three Days   28
The Visitation   29
elegy of snow   30
river religions   31
Gift Bones   33
Ghosts of the Apiary   34
Boys of Death   35
Snowfall of Stars   36
Divination of Weeds   38
Snake Handler Years   39
loam rapture   40
The Midwest Gets Drunk and Sings Along to the Radio   41
kneeling before the severed head of earth   42
Confession of Years   43
the river where the boy drowned has its seasons   44
Smoke Memories   45

Part Two

Crow Moon	49
Center of Gravity	51
Solace	52
River Birch	53
Deposition	54
Lessons in Mud	55
Six Omens in Six Days	57
Metempsychosis	58
i climbed into my body today	59
Revenant	61
Prefigured Hour	63
Mud Gospel	64
divination	65
catechism of the skull	66
Epistemology	67
Crow Theory	69
Winter Song	70
Autopsy	71
Statues	72
A History of the World	74
Fingertips	76
forgetful shadows	78
The Return	79
Unknown Music	81
Night Dance	82
Acknowledgments	83
About the Author	85

Introduction by Christopher Salerno

Judge 2024 Lena Shull Poetry Book Award

      Smoke Memories invites us into a world where memory intertwines with the natural and mystical. Where rural life illuminates the poignant resonances of family relationships. Exploring loss, grief, identity, and the inexorable passage of time, this collection, through deft poetic alchemy, transforms the ordinary into the extraordinary with its striking figurative vision. *Smoke Memories* navigates nostalgia, the cyclical nature of life and landscapes, and the haunting presence of past traumas. We come to see how the sacred and the profane can coexist in moments of loss and brutality. The poet masterfully blends narrative and lyric impulses, chasing memory into the realm of metaphor and always building some new meaning out of the fleeting and eternal facets of human existence. *Smoke Memories* offers a profound meditation on how we carry our pasts within us—memories lingering like smoke, echoing in the mind, growing in the roadside weeds, embodied by the very landscapes in which we have lived our lives. This compelling collection holds family and childhood up to the light, rendering them in ways many poetry books have not. Lucid and grave, lush and magical, *Smoke Memories* is a great book of poems.

Tomato Divination

Like a thumb smudging across the wet ink of her mind,
the doctor said. And in the weeks after that,
a cardinal began battering with territorial insistence

at our kitchen window, leaving behind, sometimes,
small offerings of blood. That this was connected
to my mother seemed to me, at age seven, as clear

as the white robes of sky. I pictured what was happening
inside her as like the mute erasure of winter snow,
or I imagined that her voice was now the dead wisteria

at the yard's edge with its poisonous seedpods, or like
the yellow jackets flying in and out of an open fissure
in the ground. And I remember my mother telling me

once before she lost herself that everything that stank
was holy: the goat droppings and goat urine in her garden,
the rake making prayerful scrapes amid manure.

And last night she returned to me out of the sky's rain,
knocking on some unseen door inside a dream—knocking
like that cardinal pecking at our window—her voice like concentric

circles inside the yellow kitchen I'd forgotten. And in her palm
was a tomato still clinging to the nub of a vine. And reaching it
toward me, she said, *These aren't store bought . . . taste.*

Part One

Orchard of Years

I keep thinking there is someone out there.
Maybe it is Mother in the dress in which

we buried her. I wonder if the gray morning light
amid the apple trees confuses her. She can't decide

where the darkness ends and the day begins.
We used to go out together and watch

the wasps getting drunk. They fed on fallen
and fermenting apples. They rolled over

on their backs and huzzed. She lifted
them and held them in her palms.

She told me once that the apple limbs sagged
not because of the burden of the globes

but because they didn't want the fruit to have
too far to drop to find the ground. And she said

that the story of Eve left out the part where
she slipped the noose around her neck and tried

to hang herself from God's cursed tree. During one
of her longest stays away, there was a view

from her hospital window of flowering crabapple
trees. I sat with her sometimes and we talked

about how the seasons were wanderers,
how they could never settle down but always,

eventually, came back home. In the car
on the ride back to the house, my father told us

that what kept happening to our mother's mind
was like the fire blight that darkened

then shriveled the leaves until they infected
every single other tree and leaf around them.

song to a raccoon on its back by the roadside

& the wind from the passing cars is a clamor
of stink

& the vultures with their blood-red heads arrive
in the anesthetic heat of morning   & soon come the plosives
of pecking

& the boys press their faces to the upstairs window

& father stands
on the back porch & studies the skewered light of day

& mother sleeps with her eyes closed like shriveled fruit

& father dreams that the twigs that hold the day moon in place
are taut as piano wires   & father imagines that the moon
will have to bite off its own leg to be free

& the moon hangs in the sky as vapor   hangs in the sky
like a bruise & a fever & a detached eye

& the raccoon sings *here is how i hold myself
in abeyance*

& the heat bullies the morning air

& the raccoon sings *here is my skin coming loose*

& the boys sing of poking the raccoon with a stick

& the vultures sing
when the cars come we will lift our bodies into air

the midwest has a few beers before church

then sits on the back porch and broods
about all the decaying leaves
waiting in the gutters

& imagines that a ladder leaned
against a house is also a ladder
leaned against the sky

or imagines fishing
in the river & watching the bobber float
as though that is the only
globe that is

& the decades seem a kind of inwardness
the hours wrapped in their dream ribbons
the breaths braiding one into the next

or maybe the midwest smokes
on the porch & that smoke
becomes a pew like a boat tied to a dock
while the preacher's words strike the hull
& say *i will unslip the knots*
of tangles in your chest

& that dead raccoon
at the roadside says
these turkey vultures
are my supplicants
& these flies will lift my prayers
& carry them

Miscarried Moon

My earliest memory is of a smear of blood
in a bathroom sink,

the horizon line of it like a sun sinking
behind the distant lip of the world.

And beside the blood was my mother's
knocked-out tooth,

its own miniature planet.
Later that summer my father took us on vacation

into the Gulf of Mexico,
and from the boat the curve of the night land

seemed its own primitive body,
something constructed out of the ossuary hours,

the skull of the moon like a chalice
from which the sea drank,

or perhaps the moon had been sliced away
from the earth

in the way my father left on the kitchen counter
the severed tails of squirrels each time

he cooked his stew. I kept my distance from the tails
in the same way I kept my distance from the tooth.

Shortsightedness

And often, it seems, we live inside the rain.
It comes to us like the folding of hands.

It moves with secret footsteps across the roof.
Or now there is that startled intake of breath

that means the years are stewing in their own
juices. My second earliest memory is of our dog

lying dead beside some railroad tracks. There is
a kind of hollowing at the center of the bones

that reminds me of a moon dragging its empty
carcass across the sky. The dog dug out

from under our fence, and I remember my mother
carrying her in her arms so we could bury

her in the backyard. Evening light is forever
a lost fire. We walk up the tracks with its tall

grass along the raised bed. We look down
the rusting and eternal lines. Something

has pulled them taut there. Something has dreamed
them out of nothing. Or maybe it is growing

dark. Or maybe the eyes cannot bring themselves
to look beyond the floaters. It rained

last night. I woke to it. I woke to its breaths
coming in through the windows to find me.

Horses in the Fog

In the slightly out-of-focus photograph,
my mother stands before her tomato plants,
the small globes behind her smudged
and indeterminate. And the cigarette at her side

lifts its smoke toward where the black blur
of a crow is caught in mid-flight above her
right shoulder, the dark creature seeming not
of this world but either coming undone

or becoming something else. And on
her left side is the kiln where she fired
clay sculptures of horses rearing up
and horses with sharp horns and horses

with the heads of dragons or serpents.
And it was beside that kiln, when I was child,
that she first described her electro-convulsive
therapies in her twenties. And it was after that,

she said, when she first began dreaming
of horses, their necks bowed in supplication
in a fog, the heavy boats of their bodies moving
across the quiet prairie sea. And she said

that the current that had gone galloping through
her brain had rearranged her thoughts into
a disordered tapestry of auguries and ungodly beasts.
And I could almost hear, as she spoke, the horseshoes

slapping mud, hear the snorts and the expelled breaths.
But, now, the sunlight in the photo seems bright
and airy on her skin, and a day moon above her
left shoulder curls into a scorpion's tail.

untitled oracle

father named us
shut up & don't push it
& you'd better hope
i don't catch you

& the light in the bedroom
my brother and i shared
grew as dense at dusk
as fertile loam

& we leaned against the windowsill
& imagined that the dimming bodies
of the clouds were broken

handkerchiefs   & the sinking sun
was a stalled & bloated wagon
floating in its blood haze

& maybe we spotted the gift
of a dead raccoon at the roadside
ghost creature

surrounded by vultures bowing
their heads
like priests

My Father, Drunk, Shakes the Apple Boughs and the Stars Fall

I remember him sitting nights on our back porch,
looking up at the sky as though the moon were a door

that was nailed shut, his hands in his lap like hibernating
creatures. And the sky was the dark tongue of a blackbird

and the stars were stalled wagons and the hours were
like the laying on of hands. Maybe my father was remembering

how his brother drowned in a river when he was nine,
while the crows, on the bank, offered their constellations of caws,

some metronome of letting go. And I wondered if
peering up at the sky while he was drunk was the only

fixity my father knew, and if the country songs
he sometimes sang cast their words into disappearing circles.

prayer for all the drunks to be our fathers

& again he places his arms around our sobbing world   &

we are his children of winter trees & yellow grass   & he whispers

words that sound as miraculous as the skinned fish of the clouds

still swimming above us in the sky   & father is the lake that turns

gray in winter & deep black at night & tender red in the suffused blood

of twilight   & if once he passed out in the shrubs past

the kitchen door   & if once he lashed out in anger with an open

palm   & if once he wept & said *sorry sorry sorry* to the moon &

we did not know to comfort him   he is still our father   still

that flickering & anguished porch light calling us home from darkness

the midwest sheds its skin

& leaves it clinging to a fence post
& that skin dreams it is a river current

or maybe the trickster light at sunset
that somehow seems a benediction

& that skin understands the martyrdom
of dead grass & it writes letters

in winter to the old snow
& those letters say *we are undone in this*

or they describe how vultures bend
their faces into roadkill

& those faces say *here is my red beard*
& once a letter fell into a stream & froze

& the ice said *i am not alone*
& sometimes the skin dreams it is

a severed possum skull with fifty teeth
left swaying from a tree limb

like a silent wind chime
& it dreams of some miraculous reassembling

dreams that if we pluck those teeth
it will somehow be a lyre

green snake reliquary

the brothers found a green snake & slapped it against
   a shagbark hickory

& the snake dreamed of its eternal loosening

& the snake thought *i have climbed down the ladder
   of my life into death*

& the brothers carried the snake into the house and left it
   beneath their sister's pillow as a reliquary

& the snake curled into the ouroboros

& the snake thought *i am every messenger of goneness*

& when their sister screamed that evening the brothers ran into
   her bedroom & waved the snake in her face & touched
   the snake to her skin & shook the snake
   back into seeming life

& that night their sister dreamed that the snake was a swollen
   tongue & a fetid river & a dark unspooling
   & a noose constricting the world's neck

& later the brothers hid the snake in her closet where it grew ripe
   & rotted like ancient fruit

& the snake said *these are my emanations*

field oracle

sister's name is *shut up*
& *go away* & *i'm warning you*
& sister imagines that the dust
on her bedroom windowsill
was once a living field
& outside her window the soybeans
lift their yellow contagion
toward the sky
then later sister follows her brothers
through the backyard
& her brothers notice her no more
than they do the dead grass along the fence
& sister sits by that fence
& sees a blind baby mouse
as hairless as a knuckle
& the stillness of that mouse says
your shadow covers my body
& the ants crawling on the mouse say
we do not forget you
& sister blows the ants
from the mouse
then lifts the creature in her hands
& her hands say
i rock you

Fourteen Omens in Three Days

The girl is watching her brothers throwing crabapples at the neighbor's cat. Watching from the upstairs window. And she watches a raccoon lying belly up on the road, two vultures with their dark shrouds of wings lifting each time a car or truck passes by. And later, when she steps out the back door and feels the soft grass beneath her feet, she looks up at a day moon left like a discarded snakeskin in the sky. And she knows this is her birthright, knows that her brothers are somewhere out there in the woods, maybe down by the river, and when they come back they will throw acorns at her head or spray her with the hose or drag her toward the open mouth of the yellowjacket nest. Once she ventured near enough that she saw the swarm moving in and out of the earth. It was primitive and ancient, like the ground itself was giving birth. And the next day, her dog leaves four bright drops of red on the kitchen floor. And the day after that, she helps her mother find horn worms on the tomato plants, and one of the tomatoes has a dark black opening in its side. In her dream that night, her brothers drown her in the river then leave her lying on the grass. In her dream, she says to her brothers, *Please*. And her brothers summon the yellowjackets that swarm around her with their dance, and the yellowjackets say, *This is your original body.*

The Visitation

An oracle of wind shuffles through dead leaves
while the boy sits in the field with the dead deer.

The quiet body makes a bed from tall grass. The quiet body
has a visitation of carrion flies. And the boy imagines

that death is made of broken earth and birdcalls, that death
casts out a line to snare each drifting cloud. And the boy

can see his house from the field, his bedroom window
and the glare of glass like bits of bone. And the deer

whispers, *Everything that lives is vaporous. Everything
that dies becomes an anthem.* And the boy imagines riding

on the dead deer's back, imagines leaping a fence
and disappearing into air. And the deer says, *The years*

arrange themselves as faint depressions in the ground.
And the deer says, *This stench of heat becomes an occultation.*

And the boy wonders if the deer will blame the snow come winter
for its motion, will blame the rain come spring for the wet drumbeat.

And the boy does not rise even when he hears his mother calling.
He lies flat and still and imagines the soft throat of decades.

elegy of snow

the boys long to kill something   to see the bright red
it makes atop the snow   a bird or a squirrel
that will offer itself to make a spectacle   & the boys
carry their pellet guns deep into the woods   & the woods
are a pale reliquary   & the woods are a cold assertion
& the brothers imagine that the snow falling around them
is restorative   & the blood they will spill will be
restorative   & their longing is like exposed rock   something
worn smooth by the tenacity of years   & the blood they imagine
is a bright blossom   is the earth's original flower   & their longing
becomes a primitive & nagging swarm inside them   & their longing
is tucked into their chests with its vague impatience
as though their hearts know only to thud themselves into this dust
& when the brothers aim their rifles at the fat squirrel perched
on the narrow limb   they envision it dropping through
the scar-tissue air   envision it twitching like an epileptic
then thumping to the frozen ground like a hammered nail

river religions

& so we blindfolded ourselves as children & grew older   & our mother

told us that life was like stepping from a bridge & falling into a river

like sinking with your arms bound   with stones in your pockets

until the river made vases from your skull to hold the flowers

& she taught us to love angled sunlight dimming into a fine smoky dust

& falling across the backyard grass   a reminder of the sacred freight

of years   the way the hours disintegrated in the fingers   & she told us

that something beautiful was coming   some wondrous good fortune

like the slow language of the cattails bending their backs in the river

& she taught us to make a potion of beardtongues & pennyworts

& bittersweets   & she told us that someday we would fall in love

& it would be like the epidendrums clinging to the trees in our backyard

& she told us how her grandfather had kept frogs & lizards in jars of formalin

& how she once had carried those jars out of the cellar & had emptied them onto

the grass   where the creatures had twitched back to life with a kind

of sorrowful epilepsy   & she told us there were signs all around us

mosquitoes levitating in the swales   auguries of loam clinging to our shoes a numerology of crows perched in the distant trees   & still we braided the days

one into the next   & still the stars were orphans in the sky

& the silence between our heartbeats became an omen or a wonder

& when certain small things in our mother's life began to disappear

when she grieved for the loss of her yellow dress   when she

despaired over a missing mud-caked pair of gardening gloves

she told us that marriage to our father was like being exiled

inside the lightness of a body that wanted only to disappear

that her days were like a river of clouds moving above her

like a liquid locomotive   & that being our mother was like the sleepy

body of the sky or the nightly flowers of the clouds or like dropping

into a river & drifting to the bottom & never getting out

Gift Bones

She—our mother—loaded them in a cardboard box
into the trunk of our Impala, where they rattled
and shifted and complained on the long drive
to Mississippi, where, upon arrival at the tiny
house outside Biloxi, we wielded shovels
in a gelatinous July heat and reburied the bones
from our three dead dogs—all loved in life, all mourned
in death—beside what would later be our mother's
flower garden, the graves marked with a clay dog
she fashioned from a potter's wheel and fired
in a kiln she had built in that new backyard,
a kiln that reminded me, whenever I surveyed it
from my bedroom window, of a miniature crematorium.
And even after we moved back to the Midwest we teased
our mother that when she died we would ferry
her bones with us wherever we went, would place
them in a cardboard box in the back of the car,
would listen to that tambourine shuffle as we drove,
though our mother insisted she would prefer we constructed
from her bones a diorama or assigned her a small cupboard
as an ossuary or whittled those bones into knitting needles
or chopsticks or daggers or back scratchers or merely
used them as cudgels, though in the end she was placed
in a full-sized crematorium, and we scattered her ashes
in the river, where they floated for a time in the current
while the bones of the clouds drifted by.

Ghosts of the Apiary

I remember my father's fingers
withdrawing the honeycomb from the hive,

remember hearing the bees buzzing
quietly with their resolute dreaming

while their tripartite bodies writhed.
And not one stung, the bees.

And the smoke silenced the air.
And the smoke boats drifted

into years until the decades whispered:
Bees like old letters in a cardboard box.

Bees floating atop a brackish pond.
And the apiary moon lists tonight

outside this window, and the bee-stars
have not one hand to hold them.

Boys of Death

sweet god of dead summer grass
& bullying sunlight where my brother

& i lay on our backs in the backyard
while insects levitated around us

& we pretended we'd been shot
in a war & had fallen to that spot

to become burning & wilting flowers
of death   & sometimes we imagined

bombs exploding around our corpses
& causing our bodies to jerk

& pirouette & bounce & come
apart & we lived inside the space

between our heartbeats & our breaths
& always when our mother called

to us to come in for supper we rose
resentfully from death & stepped inside

Snowfall of Stars

When I was in middle school, a high school boy
leapt to his death from a quarry not far from
my house, leapt either because he thought the green
eye of the water at the bottom would save him
or wouldn't. But either way I rode with my friends
on our bikes to climb the fence that had quickly
been erected, and we stood on that high perch
and marveled about a boy we had never once thought
about before, how he had stepped into the emptiness
of air like the sky was a trapdoor. That my mother
was inclined to the morbid was something I didn't
quite realize until much later in life, remembering
her fixation with matters like that human hair
was mistakenly thought to continue growing
after death, but, actually, it was the skin around
that hair that shriveled and shrank. I sat with her
often on our back porch as she drank and looked up
at the distant snowfall of stars, and we spoke
about that boy who had died and how everything
was makeshift and temporary in a life, and how
what was allotted was forever petitioned and ancient
and secretive, a wheel of being on which the body
rode. In December of that same year, she showed me
omens of deer hooves in the snow of our woods,
and we tested the indecisiveness of ice atop the river.
Its thin skin fissured and moaned as we stepped
across it. My mother told me often how she'd tried to end
her life in college, how she'd discovered something
romantic in the idea of being dead, and she told me
how, as a child, she'd liked to dress in her deceased
mother's clothes. Often, we watched crows flying
disfigured in the air above the trees. And at dusk
we studied how the weak-willed light on the horizon

appeared like a snake wending its way then discarding
some final sheath of skin. She told me often she was
hollowed out. She told me that sometimes she cultivated
madness, as if it were a recalcitrant lover. And we
lay often on our backs in the yard and gazed up
at the flotsam of stars floating in their black and bloated
sea. And sometimes we counted those specks, as though
they were a kind of numerology, and by day we counted
the crow calls, which seemed an alluvial dream beneath
a divination of clouds slipping past slowly as a hearse.

Divination of Weeds

And the boy wears his father's patience
thin by forcing them deeper into the woods—

each new step a reluctant revelation.
And the boy points toward the abandoned bricks

hidden amid the scourge of weeds. And the father
says it used to be a place of making and pronounces

it "kill." And the father shows the boy the shards
of clay bowls and saucers and cracked figurines

lying wedged amid the mud, waiting with
the forgetfulness of dropped leaves. And the father

says that someone there once summoned smoke
to rise birdlike into air, lifting into a kind of buoyant

ghostliness. And that smoke might have been sorrow
or gratitude or prayer. And the weeds around the boy

and the father are peaceful as they bend to peer into
the maw. There is a loam smell there, a smoke smell.

And the father reaches in and lifts out a small miracle
of pale bone. And fifty teeth gleam. And the boy's

father holds the possum skull like a seer. Pitiless thing.
Lost beauty from some abandoned country.

Snake Handler Years

My brother lifted a snake once from the backyard
where he had beaten it to death with a stick
then held it dangling beneath the bird-lime clouds
while a light oil of sunlight glistened beyond
his shoulder. And I have come to think that the years
tumble to the ground then decay into vinegar or commune
at night with the carrion moon, which dreams itself
amid vulturous clouds. It was a black snake
my brother held, longer than his arm, and he had
caught it on its torsional journey across the grass.
And I think often about that snake hanging limply
in his hands, and I recall the rapture of the summer
heat and envision the snake with its dangling body
that seemed to say *i am wreckage now*. And the memory
is like a vertigo of trickster light suffusing a morning
fog along a river, and it brings with it a nagging
despair like the tap tap tap of summer rain.

loam rapture

the girl who lived down the street of my childhood home
died when she was twelve & i was thirteen

though usually i picture her when she was younger
& rode a stick horse up & down her driveway

with such determination it was easy to imagine her
dreaming only of pounding hooves & snapping manes

& often i watched her from my bike or saw her fleeing
from her brothers who one july dragged her resisting

toward the pond past my father's barn & threw her in
then held her under until i feared she had drowned

which was why i assumed she so often rode that horse
in her thoughts into some faraway & imaginary field

or up into the sky to oar away with the crows
& when i was thirteen i heard the ambulance

after her uncle struck her by accident in his truck
& i saw the ambulance speeding past my father's farm

& the grass & weeds at the roadside swayed like the hooves
of an invisible horse were galloping through them

The Midwest Gets Drunk and Sings Along to the Radio

My father as he drove us drunk in his truck
would writhe like Pentecostal snakes while a heavy
hand thumped the steering wheel as he sang along
to his gospel songs and I watched the blood-red heads
of the turkey vultures perching above the dead raccoons
along the roadside. And sometimes my father drank
and sang on our back porch while I watched the wasps
getting drunk with him on the fallen apples in our yard,
their tripartite bodies small altars in the afternoon
heat as they moved with languorous slowness
then flew back to their paper hives where they engaged
in their communal hum. And still my father sang
like God was a trapdoor that might suddenly open
and send us tumbling down. And I woke some
nights to hear him arriving home and singing
as he stumbled from his truck, singing as the reverie
of a distant train horn joined him. And the words
he sang, it seemed, were like the paper skin
after the snake itself had crawled away.

kneeling before the severed head of earth

when grandfather hears the preacher speak of god's world

as a place of trumpets   as a land where eons

are carried on the backs of celestial mules   he recalls

being shot in the neck in duluth minnesota when he was nine

& when preacher speaks of faith as like the wasps that worry the fallen

apples that ferment   grandfather remembers a horse

when he was six that his father slaughtered in the snow so they could eat

& when preacher suggests that god's knuckles are the broken stations

of the cross   grandfather suspects that the preacher sees prayers

as a kind of holy emollient   that god leans down & whispers in earth's ear

& god says *i form this nest from grass & twigs*   but grandfather believes

that the sun each morning is the glowing tip of a cigarette   that the moon

is a desiccated flower   & he suspects that when god sleeps

he fears that his body is stone

Confession of Years

My mother claimed that her childhood remained forever
beyond her vision. She couldn't see it clearly

for all the warnings and regrets and omens there.
She said that the tall grass along the roadside

of her childhood home was where sorrow had invented
itself, how its very silence had learned to stir the air.

And she said that her hands had never left that place,
that they were still touching the face of her mother,

who had taught her that the deep bottom of every breath
was a contagion. My mother believed that what was wrong

with her was like plucked feathers found atop snow
in dead winter, feathers with smears of blood around them.

She confessed that the years kept devouring themselves,
insatiable in their hunger to erase. She said that a life

was like a fallen and decaying apple. And she told me once
that her mother had taken her life, which startled my grandmother,

who sat beside us in the room. And my mother told me
that the saddest light of day was when those first faint reds

set the horizon aflame with broken promises. And she added—
it was my ninth birthday—that I probably felt that way about her.

the river where the boy drowned has its seasons

& here are the cattails
that arched their backs

in a voluptuous sun
& dreamed that a neighbor boy

was a temporary weight
that a current

was the body's mantle
& that the boy's face

might dream itself back beneath
the river's ice come winter

& that spring rains might collect
like small gods

& the river would sing each day
as though to the boy's mother

*i collected your son for you
& offered him*

*to the wet & the clouds
& the birdcalls*

Smoke Memories

My mother and I were alone the night
our house burned down. I was nine that summer,
and the smell of smoke clung to my clothes.
And after the fire a tree in the yard
grew crooked with scoliosis, its back bending
away from the remains of the house.
The years that followed took on a winding
cadence, a torsional writhing like a ghost snake
muscling on its belly through tall grass. And when
I married, I knew that my memories were made
of smoke. And some days I spoke to the river
and to the stillness of the trees, and after
our son was born, I believed that to touch
his bare feet to a first snow of the season
would keep him safe, that seeing a white horse
in a dream would portend that I might die.
And some days I stood on our back porch
and studied the way the empty fields offered
their sorrowful soliloquies. And my wife
asked about that crooked childhood tree,
and I described how I would climb it every time
my father returned us to the ruins and assigned blame.
And I described for my wife how my mother and I
would sit sometimes at the back of my bedroom closet
while she smoked, how other times we escaped
outside to hide behind the tree while smoke swirled
its forgetfulness around us, and how that night,
while my father was out, she touched the tip
of one of those cigarettes to the living-room curtains
then returned to sit beside me on the couch.

Part Two

Crow Moon

I was a child
when the stars

disappeared,
and the sky grew

so dark at night
it might have been

a crow spreading
its wings.

And my mother
walked me out

to stand atop
the martyred grass,

to point above
the trees

to the abandoned
moon adrift now

in its dark sea.
And I knew

the years
were the crow

that had flown
away from us

into the sky to feed
on the seeds

of the stars,
and the moon

was just the puff
of a dandelion

ready to scatter
in the wind.

Center of Gravity

This morning arrives like a slow boat,
here with its quiet station of light

amid the clouds. We never imagine
that the world will end with vines

slowly wrapping themselves around
the sky's neck. We think we will hear

it coming, that a trumpet will
suddenly fissure air, and not that

the orator snow will fall without
a sound, fall toward the center

of everything. Once, we were fifteen
forever. There was a drumbeat inside

our chests, a weightlessness so buoyant
we were carried aloft inside our dreams

to decode the treetops. Now the years gather
like bees inside a hive, while we,

the beekeepers, perform the minor
miracles with smoke.

Solace

Our mothers lean against
the doorframe of the decades

and speak in a vigil of blue
cigarette smoke, smiling

like a cloud of bees rising
above a summer meadow.

And the light through
the windows blinds them,

and they imagine that every
heartbeat is a numerology,

that memory is forever
itinerant and vague.

But sometimes they reach
out to touch the illuminated air,

and the glow is a face
or a hand or a fluttering

or something buried so deeply
it cannot be excavated. And maybe

the smoke becomes a bird
that batters the ceilings

and walls until our mothers
whisper *hush hush*.

River Birch

And so the years of our childhood climbed aboard a wagon
and made their way into the field. And my brother and I watched
them growing smaller and smaller in the distance, shadowless
and burning, half-blind and wobbling into some original ether.
And our father's advice for most things was to suck it up.
And he told us that to wear a hat or gloves in winter was a form
of giving in, a kind of moral weakness. And once we found
our mother kneeling in bare feet by her winter garden, where nothing
grew. And that summer, fire blight claimed her lone crabapple tree,
and our father started the chainsaw then burned every branch
and withered leaf, and we watched the trunk becoming ash.
And still the years turned bitter in our throats, and we blamed
the crows and the weeds and the clouds. And our thoughts, it seemed,
arose from the trickster light of dusk and the fouled waters
of the night sky with their ghost milk of stars. And our father looked up
sometimes at those crows that waved their dark handkerchiefs against
the sky then oared out on their black boats. Though sometimes
the hours appeared to be standing still at a great distance,
waiting like a solitary river birch watching some eternal current,
as though it might be possible to construct everything from a held
breath or a memory of unblemished snow collecting in a distant
childhood meadow on a single winter day. For always there seemed
an equivalence of things: the sky became the birds became the rain
became the stars. And in the final summer of his life, our father wore
a wool sweater despite the heat, his certainty now grown brittle
around the edges, like enemy soldiers who end up, decades
following the war, laying wreaths together at a cemetery.

Deposition

My brother and I sat sometimes on our father's roof at night
and interrogated the passing clouds and the moon with its
unfathomable stillness and ossified remains. And sometimes,
by day, we walked down to the river and threw stones into
the moving current. And those stones, in the air, were planets
or meteors, and those stones, in the water, sank then disappeared.
And once, as a teenager, my brother stole flowers from
a cemetery to give to a girl he liked. And those flowers,
I remember, might have been formed from the colored sparklers
he waved in our sister's face on the 4th of July. And sometimes
I studied my mother's hands as she sat on the back porch
with our father, hands that seemed as still as small birds perching
in distant trees or clouds gathering like pallid ghosts above
the river. And sometimes what I felt inside that house was weightless
as a shadow, or like a great fire in the distance raising its odorless
and ornamental smoke, or like snow that fell soundlessly outside
a shuttered window while we slept. And there were days that became
like the names of the trees and wildflowers we learned in childhood
but soon forgot, days when we gripped our lives like a sticky door
that might fall open if only we kept tugging at it. And sometimes
when we sat on the roof, the moon tried to speak to us, saying,
*The earth is a plucked feather floating atop a becalmed
and endless sea.* And some nights, before we finally left for good,
we put down our beer cans and peed off the edge of the roof,
studying how the triumphant arcs of our sprays watered
the backyard. And that spray said, *Here is our sacred music.*

Lessons in Mud

Whenever I think of mercy,
I think of loose dirt

collecting in windowsills,
of dust rising in dry fields

to form nearly human shapes,
of the loam of river bottoms

where catfish scuff up
their small and obscuring clouds.

And I remember a copperhead
sunning itself by the garage

last spring, curled into what
seemed a kind of ghostly

contemplation, and I wonder
about the alluvium of years,

how the wet of the returning rains
makes such a prophetic mess.

My grandfather used to claim
that hoot owls late at night

expressed an inherent loneliness
of sentience, and that the spaces

between our heartbeats
were our practice at being gone.

And I used to think,
as a child, that bodies lay

in their coffins like living
vapor, like low-slung clouds

scooting low enough
to the ground to nearly touch.

In another life, we were all of us
made of wood salt and gritty

sand and topsoil. And in that
world, we imagined death

as a kind of desultory expanse,
a beautiful dirge of days

like the earthy smell
of manure on boot bottoms.

Six Omens in Six Days

This bear that keeps climbing
the oak tree outside my window
and feeding loudly on acorns

created my world when he carried me
as a child on his shoulders
up to bed or closed himself into

his office and drank himself into
a torpor and once passed out
on the back porch steps so that

my brother and I prodded him
with a foot to see if he still lived.
And there was bear scat this morning

by the tomato plants and a huff
in the bushes and the crunching
of sticks in the woods and a lightness

to the house whenever my father
wasn't in it, a buoyancy like the moon
floating on its raft across the sky

while my brother and I lay on our backs
on the roof and watched the black
bear of night keep climbing.

Metempsychosis

Plato described how Orpheus became a swan
    following death, Thamyras a nightingale, but after
our neighbor's miscarriage, the sky above her house
    transformed in the night into a dark mirror,
while the apples in her orchard fell with uncountable
    thumps, fed on by a fox we spotted sneaking
up from the river at first light. There was something
    in the way the crows called out across the hairline
of day, and something in the way that new light bruised
    the tall grass along the field's edge. I used to imagine
that years were unappeasable, that dirt grew soggy
    with rain then hardened each winter into a kind
of stone, but recently I have been wondering
    about the resurrection of wind flitting through
leaves at first light, about the skin cells of stars arriving
    after dark, about the extravagance of metaphors
we employ to describe our distillations of loss.
    Then this morning, I saw out my back window
my neighbor down on her knees by her tomato plants,
    the clouds a migration above her, her gloved hands
searching, it seemed, for hornworms. And I thought
    about the way my mother used to place tomatoes
on our kitchen windowsill to ripen. They were the size
    and shape of hearts. They had their green quietude
while angled sunlight fell through the window to expose
    the visible world. Memory is granular, I think, but in
the way that crow calls gather over years into a single ghostly
    sound, and in the way that my neighbor rose at one point
this morning to cradle a ripe tomato to her chest.

i climbed into my body today

& carried myself into the funeral home

my dad was there

bodies have always perplexed me   i think of a raft floating on a choppy sea

we hold on

or maybe our bodies are fields & we have only this botany of the self

our mud & our grass

as a child i thought sometimes about my dad's skeleton

how it waited patiently beneath his skin   hiding   & sometimes when i reached up to touch his ribs

there it was   the hard comfort & reality of bone

i was nine the first time he almost died

the honda went off the road

& i was sitting beneath a gathering of stars while they lifted him

& my dad used to carry me on his shoulders

& i would duck so as not to bump my head

& he had an adam's apple too large for his throat

a living thing longing to get out   that quivered when he spoke

& my dad used to say *first rotate your hips   which rotates your shoulders   that's how you hit a homerun*

& the second time my dad almost died it was a heart attack

he was up on a roof when it happened   giving an estimate to repair a leak

& we sat in his hospital room & felt guilty that our bodies functioned

& it was raining this morning when we woke

& that rain fell against the body of the house

& more rain fell against the body of the car as we made our way to the funeral home

& more rain fell against the bodies of our umbrellas as we made our way across the parking lot

then stepped inside

& my dad was there

& i said when i reached down to touch him

dad

Revenant

My father's boots remained
leaning against the barn

the winter after he died,
stiff with cold, dream

boots beneath a hollow
sky. The days undressed

themselves and became
the naked trees lifting

their arms toward the marbled
muscles of the clouds.

My father had lost part of an index
finger as a boy, and he liked

to say he could tell a storm
was coming whenever

that missing digit throbbed.
I wondered about that finger

sometimes when I studied
the boots from my bedroom

window, one upright
and the other toppled

on its side, snow sometimes
falling around them but never

covering them completely.
And I dreamed one night

that an owl lifted those
boots in its talons

and carried them to a nest
high into a distant tree,

and inside that nest
was my father's finger.

In the spring, my brother
and I carried the boots

to the river and made
a somber ceremony of dropping

them from the train bridge,
expecting them to float off

like ghostly rafts, but they
sank at once then disappeared.

And from then on whenever
we crossed that bridge,

we looked down and imagined
that a boot was a finger

was a river was an owl
was a father was death.

Prefigured Hour

And the boys imagine their father is the snake that lives
beneath the porch and curls into the ouroboros.

And the brothers lie on their bellies on the grass,
and the snake lies on its belly, too, silent in the dirt.

And the boys imagine their father is the boots
he left by the back door, caked with the world's mud,

that their father is the crow lying still at the road's verge,
some dark obelisk formed in stuporous morning light.

And the boys suspect their father is the film of dust
on the windowsill and the gray fog lingering above the river.

And sometimes he is the myopia of grass and the broken
earth and the wet smell of leaves in heavy rain.

And their father is the pilgrimage of hours, and the boys
imagine each day's eyelid slowly opening and closing

while a hearse of clouds moves past like a parade,
And their father is the smoke seeping from a neighbor's chimney

and gathering itself into a kind of living breath, floating above
the caretaker trees amid the evening calls of crows.

And the boys believe their father swims now with the catfish
and is some unknown map and augury of shadows.

Mud Gospel

And he spoke to us in our dreams after he was gone.
Talked to us in his truck and at the kitchen table and on
the back porch when the stars were meditating above the barn,
and his words were cudgels and brushfires and a wail of sirens.
And he talked while he knelt over a dead doe and sliced the knife blade
from sternum to crotch and while he carried us as boys up the stairs
to bed. And sometimes his voice was a cadence and a drum and a gospel,
and sometimes the words perched with the crows or muscled
out on their bellies with the snakes or skinned themselves of their
flesh to make the moon. And once he left the footprints of his words
in the deep snow in the backyard, and often he wrote his words in
the miraculous bodies of the clouds, and in death he spoke in a priest
of light falling through the kitchen window, in the smell of woodsmoke,
in the small gods of fireflies blinking on and off on summer nights.
And we carried the words in the deep backs of our throats and in
the myopia of years we ferried on our backs and in the deep recesses
of our pockets where we sorted through them often like loose change.

divination

after she learned so long ago that she was newly pregnant
she must have dreamed one night
that her sons were crows & slipped free
from her body on their black boats
& oared across the evening sky
& that their wings were oars
& they were calling out
with a kind of feral faraway
& because of the years of miscarriages
she woke thinking of bees emerging
from a slit in the backyard grass
& she imagined that the boys
waiting inside her were divinations
& she pictured them running
beneath a membrane of sky amid
the crested yellow heads of soybean fields
& pictured that soon her boys
would be boy flesh & boy smells
& her boys come winter would watch
the snow coming down
& their breaths would say
here is the body's partition
& their breaths would say
the snow speaks to us in quiet voices
& soon the years would insist
on their own silent syncopation
& the boys would gaze at the snow & pray
& their prayers would say
come embrace this land
with your body

catechism of the skull

i have been thinking about these sidelong glances
toward the abyss that awake us in the night

while crickets claim dominion   & it seems
that the bucket of the world is forever full
& nothing is more dreamlike than a shard

of moon buried in the sky's mud outside
a bedroom window   & in these ebbtides

of sleep there is only sensibility & quiet
questions & we live in our original bodies
like the skull i keep atop my bookshelf

a possum skull that waddled once with its pale
moon face & its fifty teeth & its prehensile tail

that gripped the living world   my mother
took me as a child to mississippi to visit
her younger sister who was dying of breast cancer

& who wore a wool sweater in the dense heat
& we stood one evening before a placid

gulf of mexico that seemed a sleepy
& forgetful gray god   & two decades
later my mother's own diagnosis made

those intervening years seem like the hinge
of bat wings fluttering erratically above

the lawn at night when my brother & i
were kids & we would toss tennis balls into
the air to see if they would chase them

Epistemology

When the boy who used to place me repeatedly in headlocks
on the school bus then punch me with his free hand died

last fall, his obituary listed the names of his children
and grandchildren, an almost-biblically impressive collection

of begetting. And as I read those names in the paper,
I remembered the tireless pistons of the boy's blows

existing in the same continuity of time as the evening he had
his mother phone my mother to see if I would spend the weekend

at his farm, because—or so my mother claimed—he said I was
his closest friend in the world. I returned to these thoughts

yesterday while driving home from Dayton, and thought, too,
how my father had similarly confused affection and violence,

and how he told me once that the only constant of the world
was that everyone was forever trying to fuck over everyone else,

which he presented as the one true economic lesson, a justification,
I came to understand, for his own bad behavior. All of these

memories led to still another of how my dad used to drive me
sometimes to a mall that later was bulldozed down to nothing,

and how once—after its destruction—I rode my bike there
with my brother to throw stones and to marvel at what wasn't,

though soon we crossed the road to the Dairy Hut and imagined
with a strange pleasure that the mall had been destroyed by

falling bombs, which had transformed its general goneness
into a kind of beautiful ugliness, elevated in that moment,

especially when geese on their passage south began squawking
above the remains, the sounds expressing a communal solitude

or maybe an otherworldly lamentation beneath parasitic clouds.
But all those thoughts vanished, of course, the very instant on

the ride home from Dayton when a sudden wall of snow drifted
its indeterminacy across I-75, making a blankness of the world,

and I didn't know whether to brake or to continue on ahead,
though I saw, for the briefest of moments when the curtain opened,

a car in front of me twisting to aim the other way, skidding on
the ice, the face of the driver locked in a wild gaze. Then the white

kicked up again to cloak us, and I didn't know whether this time
it might somehow form itself into a shape or an idea or a language

or a belief, or if the world itself had somehow flickered out,
reducing everything everywhere to this unknowing.

Crow Theory

The feather the boy finds in the woods
is made of black stillness.

And the boy imagines the feather
is his father. And the boy carries it

into the house and hides it beneath his pillow.
And at night he envisions a crow lifting itself

on its mud wings beneath the floating clouds.
And the crow says, *This is my dark decay.*

And the crow says, *I am a floating bier.*
And when the boy wakes, he pretends

that his father is the first pink light above the barn,
that the days are hammered thin as the low fields

over which each pale day drifts. And he believes
that his memories of his father are like a ladder

rising up and up to touch the clouds. And sometimes
he pretends that the months are a vapor

atop the river and that the years move out on
the musculature of their bellies. And he imagines the crow

floating on the eyelid of a morning moon.
And he hears a living bird calling by the barn,

and its music is a cold thing and a metronome
and something primitive formed from mud.

Winter Song

The ice atop the river where the neighbor boy
drowned is sometimes covered with snow

and sometimes not. And the parasitic moon
at night seems a wide-eyed dirge. And sometimes

we see the parents in their backyard gazing
toward the river's empty inventory, and there are

deer tracks most early mornings in the snow, tracks
that appear then disappear, ghost creatures that can't

make up their minds if they exist. And there is
a sound the wind makes while it skitters over

hardened snow, a sound like a cough at the deep
back of a throat, a rattle or a wail. And today there is

an augury of bruised blue-gray light as we rise,
and the falling snow appears unmoored.

Autopsy

The winter my father became antlers,
it snowed so often overnight I expected

nothing but white. But there were
blood drops in the woods, hoof prints

shaped like gouged triangles. My father
carried me often like a dead deer

on his shoulders up the stairs to bed,
my arms and legs gripped before his body,

my fallen neck bobbing. The eyes
were lacquered black whenever he ferried

the creatures into the yard and dropped them
on the snow. And the stars some nights

were ovaries. And the moon was an albino
testicle. Antlers, he told me, could grow up

to half an inch a day. My father knelt
as a priest before the body, knelt with

ceremonial devotion as he ran the knife
from sternum to crotch, creating a benediction

of what fell out. And once he shot a ten-point
and mounted the antlers on his head.

And he jabbed them at my mother, who told me
to always back away from a deer in rut.

And the winter he died, we glued
his antlers to the basement wall.

Statues

I used to watch the old men
fishing sometimes in the river
behind the house, the stillness
of their bodies an inventory,

like they were counting down
the few years they had left.
And sometimes the old men held
their fishing poles like divinations,

and the tops of their heads were like
grass turning pale and desiccated
with winter, annulled by snow.
And I wondered if they could feel

the end approaching, if they could hear
it whispering with the cattails pressing
against each other in the current.
And sometimes I pictured mosquitoes

anointing their skin in blood, pictured
the men restless at night and peering out
their windows at the parasitic stars.
And I could not believe I would ever

grow that old, would ever stand by a river
while the last vulture-light amid the trees
turned the world a dusky sludge.
Now, of course, I wake nights to remember

how those men—long dead—watched
for the torsional bodies of the fish
while believing it was possible
to linger like a cut flower in a vase.

A History of the World

When my grandmother opened the drawstring
pouch she'd lifted from her jewelry box, I imagined

a cloud unfurling its belly and releasing hail. I was nine.
This was Escanaba. Teeth tumbled forth. Rolled atop

the dresser. Later, I would think that sound
was like the thin skin of ice cracking and fissuring

on Little Bay de Noc the morning we walked out
too early in the season, the landscape around us slowly

emerging from the primitive ether of the fog.
Often, when we visited, I woke to the augury

of invisible crows calling warning from the unknown
woods behind the barn. In winter, the black of the bodies

against snow stood out in the way one darkened smear
of blood clung to a tooth my grandmother pushed

toward me with a finger. If the clouds at night were
the uncut hair of the dead, the baby teeth of my father's

younger brother—who died during the Depression
after a fall from a barn, who died at almost the exact

age as when I first saw his teeth—seemed like the broken
wheel of history. I could picture a wagon creaking

and wobbling into some misty eternity of decades. And when
my grandmother died, the teeth were passed down

to my father, who kept them in his desk drawer,
still secreted inside that same purple pouch. I sneaked in

sometimes to roll the teeth in my fingers or to cast
them across his desktop like miniature dice. Here was

a numberless numerology. Here was the sound
of a world coming into being. And once, I carried

the teeth to school to show my friends, to hold
in my palm the hardened history of everything.

Fingertips

Early morning light seems more faint and fragile these days,
like it is practicing becoming a ghost

or is reaching its fingers like new roots
into barren dirt that will not have it.

And still the neighbors fight so loudly some nights
that their voices pause into a small afterlife

between our houses. I lived there once, lived inside
a density of agitated air that knew

only its own vibrations.
Arguing is probably just another way of remembering,

not the details but the shape of an hour
or a year or the way a tree contorts its back sometimes

to find the sky. There is a permanence to certain ways
of letting go, which I think about some cold nights

while watching smoke lifting from neighboring chimneys,
the swirling grays

forming dark cloudflowers I know exist only inside the body
of the temporary world.

When my mother was dying, I listened to the metronome
of her breaths, which seemed

a numerology, some counting out of what could not be known
except that it had its own imperatives.

And these days I rise early and walk out into a wraith of air
that knows to hold its breath, and I look over

to the house where my neighbors perhaps lie sleeping
contentedly arm in arm in the fingertips of day.

forgetful shadows

after his mother took her life   the boy imagined
that there was a slowness to the shadows

crossing the yard outside her bedroom window
& a vague impatience to the moonlight

& once he dreamed that his mother
was a snakeskin clinging to a wire fence

& that the hours showed their ribs
like a coyote trotting low slung & forgetful

across a dusk field   & once his mother
had watched them lifting a green snake by the tail

& holding it wriggling before them
like a living occultation   & often

they had walked together to study
the muddy passage of the river   to study

in winter the ice that made of the river's skin
something as hard & unforgiving as stone

but now the boy's mother is a screech owl
in the night   is the decomposing sound

of rain against the roof   & always
when the boy wakes in the morning

he imagines his mother with her eyes closed
& holding her breath inside the grave

The Return

My dead are sitting with me again this morning
on my back porch and saying nothing

beneath the berried clouds and the brightening
mouth of day, the unperturbed backyard

grass wearing the dun robes of forever.
I feel a certain short-sightedness in the chest,

as complicit as the tufts of weeds claiming
the neglected vegetable garden. And my dead

sit wordlessly around this table while I gaze out
at the pale throat of eons. And if the stars

last night wore the sky as their burial wrappings,
this morning the light pools amid the waking birds,

the flesh of day opening to let the years spill out.
My lungs know only to draw in this air then let it go,

in the way the years come toward me now then disappear,
in the way I used to imagine as a child prayers

rising through the church rafters to get snared
in the tree limbs or the clouds. I used to sit in those

hard pews like a boy condemned, my hair slicked
back and my shirt top button so tight at my throat

it was a garrote. But now the alluvium of night
has given way to the bloodied entrails of the clouds,

and deer in the distance seem waxen
into stupor, their heads bowed in supplication.

Unknown Music

We know it waits there in the cradle
of the sky. Waits amid the scars of clouds
with their thickets of white. My mother
spoke often of the kingdom, as though
it were possible to trace the path of birds
into a tapestry. There is a language of dark
and a language of light, and neither
knows the other until they are the same.
The first song, I think, was death,
and it brushed against our legs in the tall
grass, and we named it for the gates
that kept opening and closing in our dreams,
named it for the dust-colored passage
of the years. Even decades dissolve
on the tongue. My mother told me once
that stars were fireflies that blinked on
and off so slowly we never noticed,
told me that my father was the day's
last light the sun cast on a river's surface.

Night Dance

My sister wears our dead mother's dresses
in my dreams. Wears moonlight in her hair.

And once she wears a single black feather as the sky.
And so the days paralyze themselves,

and the years grow sluggish then forgetful.
And soon, a broken spine of morning

falls through a window. A penance made
of hard dirt or frozen snow come winter.

And still the dresses twirl amid the undergrowth,
dance shadowless, entangled. And the dresses say,

Here are my dark velocities. And sometimes
my sister closes her eyes and hears the dresses

fanning out to make a shroud, and sometimes
our mother lifts her arms and turns.

Acknowledgments

Grateful acknowledgment is made to the editors of the following publications where the poems in this collection were originally published.

Alaska Quarterly Review: "Orchard of Years" and "Tomato Divination."
Allium, A Journal of Poetry & Prose: "the midwest has a few beers before church."
Asheville Poetry Review: "Confession of Years."
Barrow Street: "Fingertips."
Beloit Poetry Magazine: "i climbed into my body today."
Briar Cliff Review: "elegy of snow."
Chautauqua: "Metempsychosis," "The Return," and "Six Omens in Six Days."
Cider Press Review: "Shortsightedness" and "The Visitation."
December: "Crow Theory" and "Horses in the Fog."
DMQ Review: "Fourteen Omens in Three Days"
Gulf Coast: "Autopsy."
The Inflectionist Review: "Night Dance" and "Solace."
I-70 Review: "Deposition," and "Snowfall of Stars."
Louisiana Literature: "Crow Moon" and "forgetful shadows."
Narrative Magazine: "The Midwest Gets Drunk and Sings Along to the Radio," "prayer for all the drunks to be our fathers," and "Statues."
Nimrod International Journal: "Gift Bones" and "Boys of Death."
Pedro River Review: "Winter Song."
Pleiades: "field oracle."
Plume: "the midwest sheds its skin."
Prairie Schooner: "Mud Gospel" and "Revenant."
RHINO: "catechism of the skull."
The Shore: "untitled oracle."
South Carolina Review: "River Birch."
South Florida Poetry Journal: "divination," "Divination of Weeds," "Ghosts of the Apiary," "green snake reliquary," "loam rapture," and

"the river where the boy drowned has its seasons."
Southern Humanities Review: "Center of Gravity."
The Southern Review: "A History of the World" and "river religions."
Spectrum Literary Journal: "song to a raccoon on its back at the roadside."
The Sun: "Smoke Memories."
Sycamore Review: "kneeling before the severed head of earth."
Tahoma Literary Review: "Prefigured Hour."
Talking River Review: "Miscarried Moon."
Terrain.org: "Unknown Music."
Thrush Poetry: "My Father, Drunk, Shakes the Apple Boughs and the Stars Fall."
TriQuarterly: "Epistemology."
Valparaiso Poetry Review: "Midsummer Grass" and "Snake Handler Years."
Willow Springs: "Lessons in Mud."

About the Author

Doug Ramspeck is the author of ten poetry collections, two collections of short stories, and a novella. Individual poems have appeared in journals that include *The Southern Review, The Missouri Review, Kenyon Review, Slate, The Sun,* and *The Georgia Review*. He lives in Black Mountain, North Carolina. His author website can be found at dougramspeck.com.

Made in the USA
Middletown, DE
16 February 2025